Blue blanket	Mother Moo	A happy gator	The pink witch	Get a haircut			You just got wet
Surfing fish	Pig with fruit	Porthole fishing	Green rug	Banner with jug	Fruit cart	Pie	Fountain
Sea monster	Cannonballs	Through the door	Rescued	Blunderbuss	Crow's nest	Guard the treasure	Figurehead
Pull the bucket	Keep digging	Pointed tail	Watch out	Sir Gator	Treasure map	Hold on tight	Monster fish
Falling	The sad dragon	The torch	The smiling dragon	The drawbridge	Hanging onto a rope	The resting dragon	The way out
Broken sword	The guard is sleeping	Bowling	Robinfox	Climbing up	Sword and shield	Helping a friend	Very lazy
Attack	Caught in a net	Throw it out	Sir Bluefox	Not very happy	The escape	A spy at the window	Sir Doofus
Farmer	Look at that	Tell a story	The purple wizard	A singing elephant	Roll the keg	One small raccoon	The grand crown
Bird's nest	Draw a picture	The fence	Hammering	Pear basket	Pitcher and cup	A hiding bunny	He stole the eggs
Hiding in the bushes	The magic sword	Bluebird	School is out	Catch the ball	Read a book	Come inside	Up at bat

This book is dedicated to
all of my children.

Zebulon, Benjamin, Arden, Jessie,
Len, Uncle Ben, Uncle Agget,
and
children yet to come

A Green Frog Publishers Inc. / J. R. Sansevere Book

LITTLE CRITTER®
IN SEARCH OF
THE BEAUTIFUL PRINCESS
❧ BY MERCER MAYER ❧

THE GREAT HALL

Once upon a time in a far away land in a grand castle lived a brave knight. His name was Sir Bunnylot. Squire Critter thought Sir Bunnylot was the bravest and strongest knight in all the land. On the day of the Great Feast, 101 blackbirds flew into the hall. One of the blackbirds had a letter. And the letter read: Help!!! Please rescue me.

Signed by
The Beautiful Princess

Can you find Sir Bunnylot?
Can you find Squire Critter?
Can you find the blackbird with the letter?

THE CASTLE

Sir Bunnylot and Squire Critter went to bed early. The next day they were going to rescue the Princess. But no one else in the castle was sleepy. Somewhere a minstrel was playing and singing very loudly.
The blackbird who delivered the letter decided to stay for a while.

Can you find Sir Bunnylot?
Can you find Squire Critter?
Can you find the blackbird?
Can you find the minstrel?

OUTSIDE THE CASTLE

The next morning Sir Bunnylot was very grumpy because he had lost his brand new yo-yo.
So Squire Critter drew a picture on Sir Bunnylot's flag and shield just to cheer him up.
They did not know that a spy sent from the castle of the evil Green Knight was lurking in the bushes.

Can you find Squire Critter?
Can you find Sir Bunnylot's flag?
Can you find Sir Bunnylot's shield?
Can you find Sir Bunnylot?
Can you find Sir Bunnylot's yo-yo?
Can you find the spy?

THE FOREST

Sir Bunnylot and Squire Critter set off through the forest to rescue the Princess. Suddenly, they were surrounded by bandits. To make matters worse, Sir Bunnylot dropped his sword somewhere. They had even lost their frying pan. Now, how were they going to cook breakfast on their journey?
But all was not lost. Sir Hogwash came to the rescue.

Can you find Sir Bunnylot?
Can you find Squire Critter and Sir Bunnylot's sword?
Can you find Sir Hogwash?
Can you find the frying pan?
Can you find this bandit?

THE TOURNAMENT

Sir Hogwash saved the day. He invited Squire Critter and Sir Bunnylot to the Royal Tournament. All the knights in the Kingdom were jousting to see who would rescue the Princess. Sir Bunnylot was next to joust. He had his lance, but his sword was still lost. That made him very grumpy indeed.

Lady LaBelle took one look at Sir Bunnylot and fell madly in love. She gave him her scarf to wear as a good luck charm. Close by, another one of the Green Knight's spies was watching and waiting.

Can you find Squire Critter?
Can you find Sir Bunnylot?
Can you find Lady LaBelle?
Can you find the spy?

THE ENCHANTED FOREST

Squire Critter went to look for Sir Bunnylot's sword, but he got lost. Luckily, a Fairy told Squire Critter of a magic sword which was stuck in a stone deep in the forest. "I'll just borrow the sword. I'm sure no one will mind," said Squire Critter. That part of the forest was full of enchanted creatures, but it didn't bother Squire Critter one bit. He was very brave.

Can you find the magic sword?
Can you find the Fairy?
Can you find Squire Critter?
Can you find a unicorn?

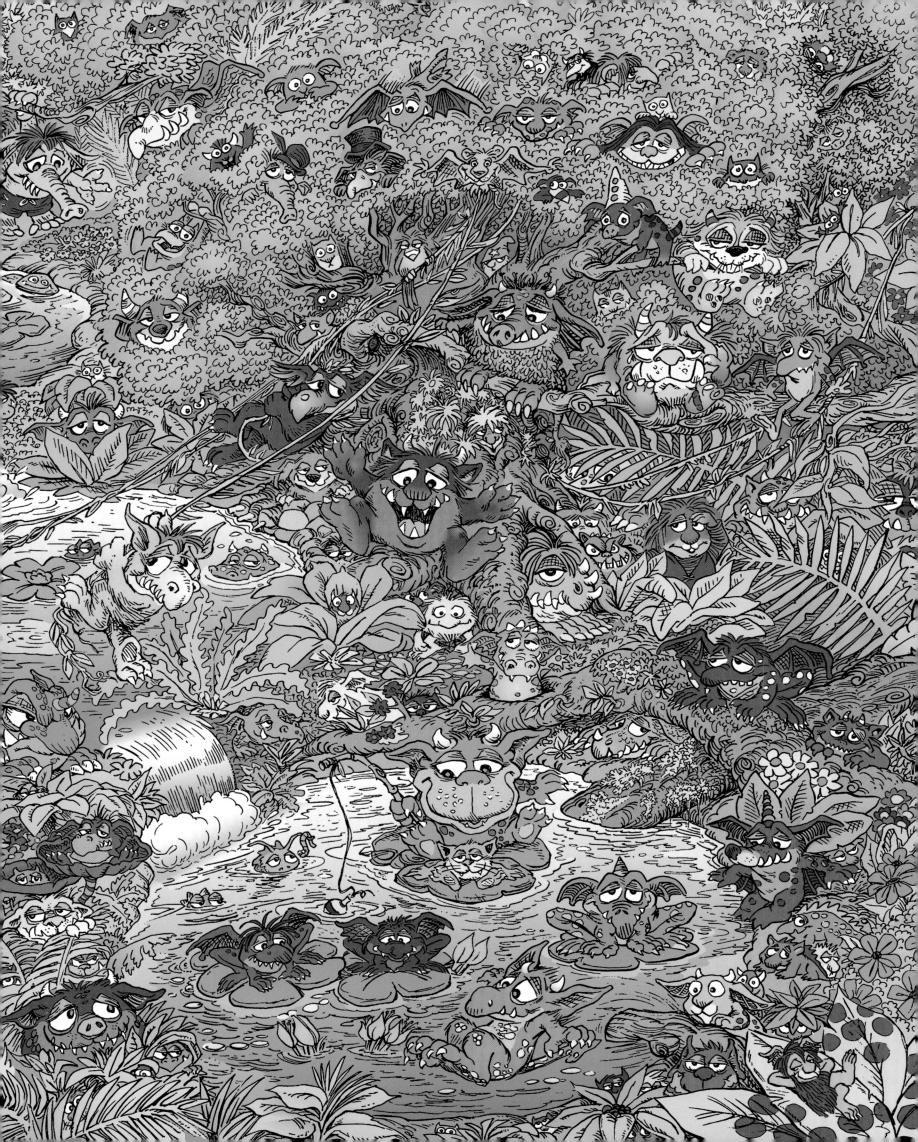

THE VILLAGE

As Squire Critter tried to pull the enchanted sword from the stone, the sword turned into a red rose. Squire Critter carried the rose back to the village to show Sir Bunnylot. Everywhere he looked there was food for sale. Boy, was he hungry. Two spies sent by the Green Knight were hiding in the village. They were watching Squire Critter very carefully, but he was too hungry to notice.

Can you find Sir Bunnylot?
Can you find Squire Critter and the rose?
Can you find the two spies?
Can you find an apple with a worm?

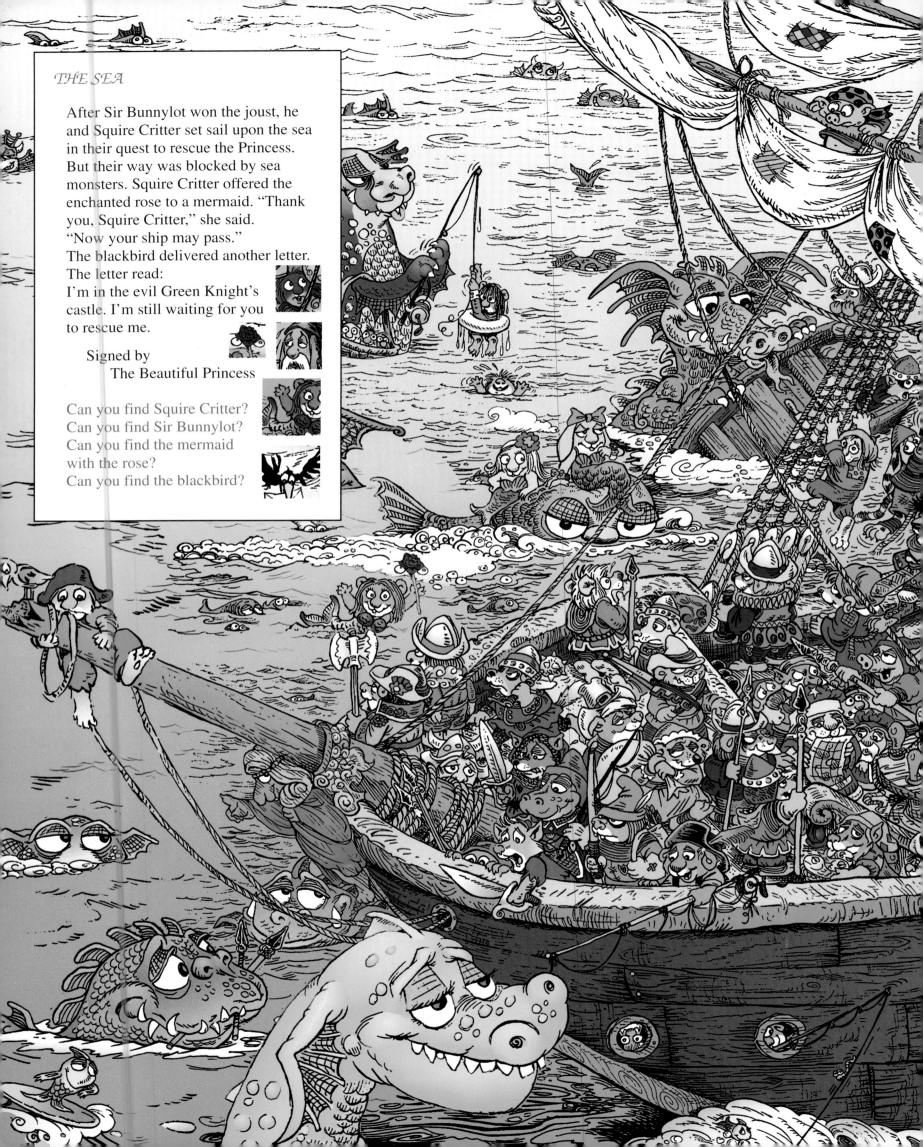

THE SEA

After Sir Bunnylot won the joust, he and Squire Critter set sail upon the sea in their quest to rescue the Princess. But their way was blocked by sea monsters. Squire Critter offered the enchanted rose to a mermaid. "Thank you, Squire Critter," she said.
"Now your ship may pass."
The blackbird delivered another letter. The letter read:
I'm in the evil Green Knight's castle. I'm still waiting for you to rescue me.

Signed by
    The Beautiful Princess

Can you find Squire Critter?
Can you find Sir Bunnylot?
Can you find the mermaid with the rose?
Can you find the blackbird?

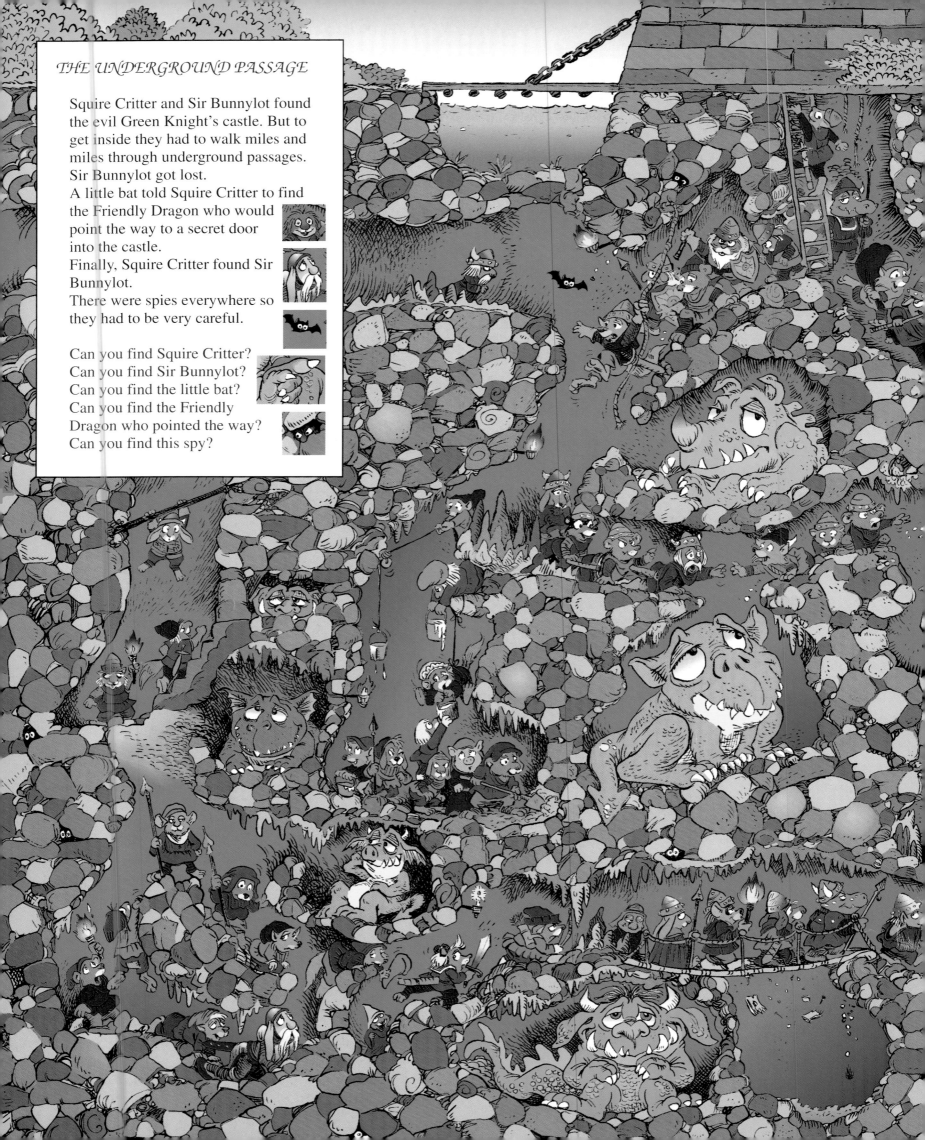

THE UNDERGROUND PASSAGE

Squire Critter and Sir Bunnylot found the evil Green Knight's castle. But to get inside they had to walk miles and miles through underground passages. Sir Bunnylot got lost.

A little bat told Squire Critter to find the Friendly Dragon who would point the way to a secret door into the castle.

Finally, Squire Critter found Sir Bunnylot.

There were spies everywhere so they had to be very careful.

Can you find Squire Critter?
Can you find Sir Bunnylot?
Can you find the little bat?
Can you find the Friendly Dragon who pointed the way?
Can you find this spy?

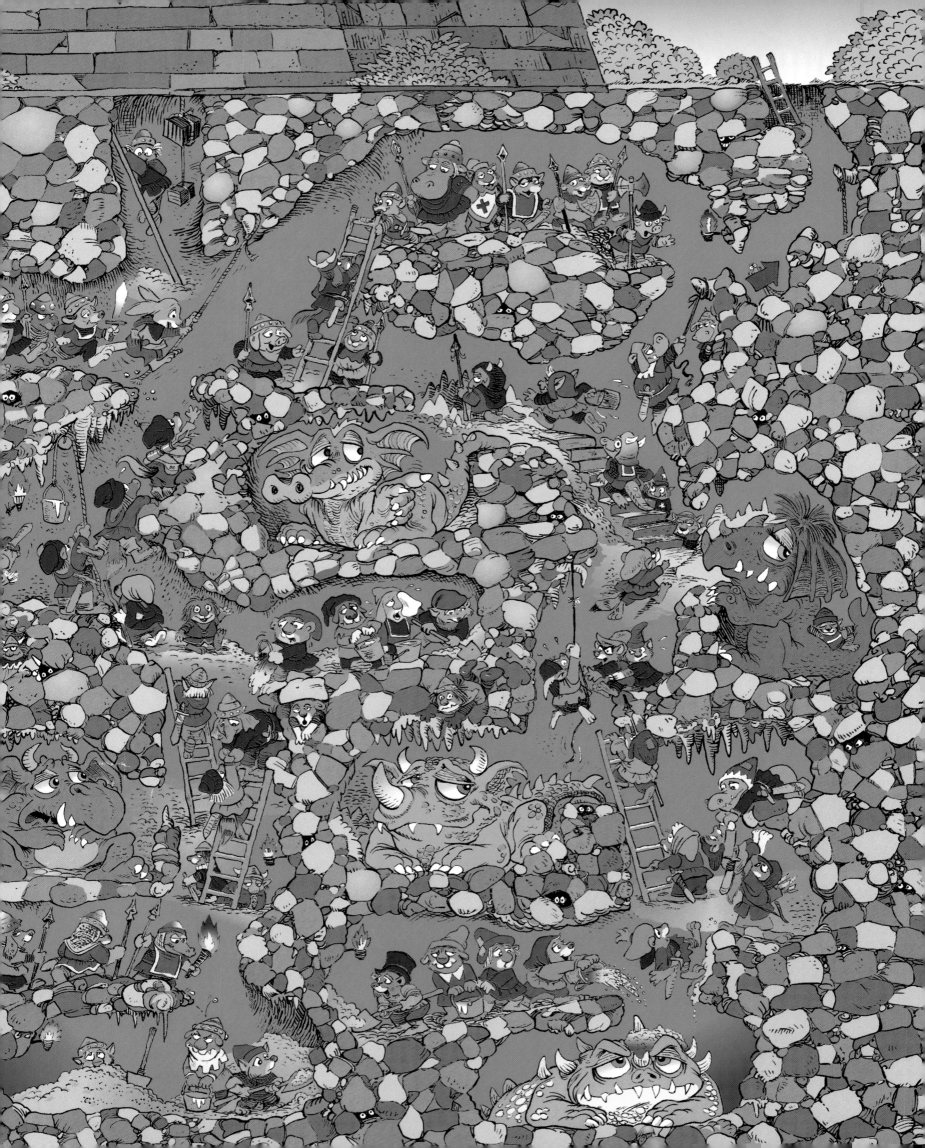

THE GREEN KNIGHT'S CASTLE

Squire Critter and Sir Bunnylot crept through a secret door into the Green Knight's castle. It was time for the big battle, but Sir Bunnylot tripped and bumped his head. The evil Green Knight was having sword practice with his soldiers. His cook had just baked his favorite pie. He left in a hurry, so he could eat the whole pie by himself. The Green Knight was very selfish and never liked to share.

Meanwhile Squire Critter was looking for the Princess.

The Princess was hoping to catch a glimpse of the famous Prince who had been turned into a frog and was living somewhere in the castle courtyard.

Can you find Sir Bunnylot?
Can you find Squire Critter?
Can you find the evil Green Knight?
Can you find the Princess?
Can you find the frog Prince?
Can you find the pie?

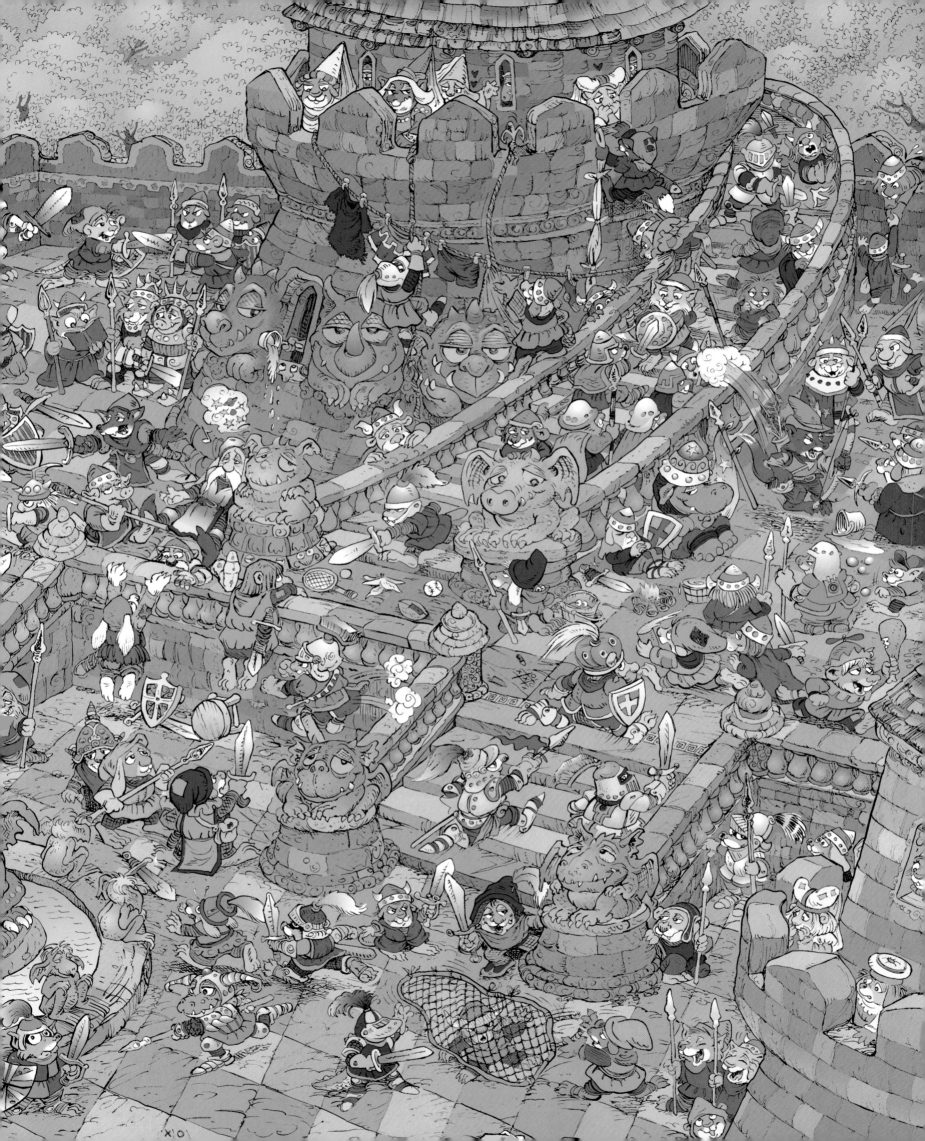

THE CELEBRATION

Squire Critter rescued the Princess. The King and Queen decided to make him a knight. Everyone came for the celebration, except for the evil Green Knight who had a tummy ache.
All through the Kingdom, bells rang for Squire Critter, who was nowhere to be found. Squire Critter was just too tired from so many adventures.
But best of all, Sir Bunnylot's yo-yo had finally been found.
Can you find it?
            And
Can you find Squire Critter?
Can you find Sir Bunnylot?
Can you find the Fairy?
Can you find Sir Hogwash?
Can you find the
        Friendly Dragon?
Can you find the Princess?

BACK AT SCHOOL

The school bell rang. Little Critter woke up. He had been sleeping at his desk. Now it was time to go home. "Oh no," said Little Critter. "It was just a dream."
Sir Bunnylot was really Little Critter's teacher.
Sir Hogwash was really the librarian.
The Green Knight was the principal.
And the Beautiful Princess was really Little Sister.
But if it was just a dream, then why was the Fairy from the enchanted forest visiting Little Critter's school?

Can you find Little Critter?
Can you find his teacher?
Can you find the librarian?
Can you find the principal?
Can you find Little Sister?
Can you find the Fairy?

Can you find all of these?

Jester pig · The throne · Hanging on · Gator guard · Blackbird with rose · Unhappy hippo · Jester cat · Lady on the stairs

Turkey dinner · Headless knight · Fruit basket · Her Royal Hipponess · The cookie cook · The hidden mirror · An elephant guard · The window lamp

Bags of gold coins · Lady Foxflower · Flag in the wind · You are in jail · The wheelbarrow · Hiding in a tent · Barrel down the stairs · Hippo guard

Hang it on the wall · Have a snack · Fried eggs · Cut the cloth · Guess who? · The ax · A juggler · A gate tower

Having a nap · A magic carrot · Smile three times · Master Sergeant Oink · Strange stuff · Filling the jug · The falcon shield · A laughing kitty

Three bandits · You may hide · The trap · Climb the tower · Rhino lookout · Hanging upside down · Hiding in the straw · The charge

The yellow flag · Grandpa · The spyglass · Bandits are coming · Up the rope ladder · From the rope bridge · A mace · A wise wizard

Sing a song · Throw down the glove · Run away · Wave at a friend · The helmet · Surprise · Flags on tents · Cover your eyes

The boot · A zigzag flag · The joust begins · The Flying Whizzo · A Banded Beaksnook · Tame Sunblurp · The Fishing Mudgump · Wild Sneets

A Frogitroid · A Howling Treefus · A Blupinator · A Red Noseeum · A Dragonette · A Doodlecoot · A Hatted Wiggly · Old Foopeedoo